How To Make Your Theatre Pay

A comedy

David Henry Wilson

Samuel French—London
New York-Toronto-Hollywood

FOR AMATEUR PRODUCTION ENQUIRIES

UNITED KINGDOM AND WORLD
EXCLUDING NORTH AMERICA
plays@samuelfrench.co.uk
020 7255 4302/01

Each title is subject to availability from Samuel French,
depending upon country of performance.

HOW TO MAKE YOUR THEATRE PAY

First performed by The Wessex Actors Company in March 1998, with the following cast:

Rouse	Magnus Stewart
Mike	Gary McKinven
	(later replaced by Julian Chaloner)
Mavis	Angela Touhig

Directed by Pat Hudson

The first London production was at the Union Theatre in May 1999, with the following cast:

Rouse	Jamie Neil
Mike	Kieran Buckeridge
Mavis	Abigail Fisher

Directed by Nick Pilton

CHARACTERS

Rouse, small, seedy, obnoxious. He has a sort of semi-educated accent, with flattened vowels: he pronounces his name "Riouse", "name" becomes "naeem" etc. Final "l" sounds turn into "w"; "Council" is thus "Ciounciw". And "people" becomes "peopwe"

Mike, pleasant, well-spoken

Mavis, very sexy, and revealingly dressed

The action of the play takes place on the stage of a theatre. The onstage set can, therefore, be anything at all

Time — the present

HOW TO MAKE YOUR THEATRE PAY

The stage of a theatre

*When the play begins, Mike Pemberton-Hawkesley is inspecting the
set. Mavis is in the auditorium as a member of the audience*

Rouse enters

Rouse Mr Pemberton-Hawkesley?

Mike Yes.

Rouse Rouse is the name. From the Council. We had an appointment
for one o'clock.

Mike Oh yes!

Rouse And it's now eleven and a half minutes past one, which
emolumates a loss of eleven and a half minutes.

Mike I'm sorry, I'd forgotten you were ...

Rouse A lot of people forget that I'm coming, but I come all the
same.

Mike What can I do for you, Mr Rouse?

Rouse The question is what I can do for you, Mr Pemberton-
Hawkesley. I've been asked by the Chairman of the Council, my
very good friend Sir Charles, to try and turn your substantial
losses into something more acceptable to the Council. Namely, a
profit.

Mike Well, that would be nice.

Rouse Not merely nice, Mr Pemberton-Hawkesley. Indecrundible.
Let's start with this name of yours, shall we?

Mike My name?

Rouse Extremely uneconomical.

Mike I'm sorry. I happen to have been born with it.

Rouse Then change it. If we all stuck to what we were born with, we should never leave our mother's nipples. However, I am not here to huggle over your name or your mother's nipples. I shall call you Pem, which at a stroke is a saving of eighty-seven and a half per cent. Rouse researches have revealed that the average head of department is addressed by name at least twenty-four times a day, which at a saving of one second per call will indentrify two minutes saving in a five-day week, or one hundred and four minutes per year, or just under seventeen and a half hours in ten years.

Mike Everybody calls me Mike.

Rouse Oh! Am I to take it that you are on first-name terms with your employees?

Mike Certainly. Aren't you?

Rouse Absolutely not. Inferiors must be kept in their place. First name today, give me a rise tomorrow. No, no, Pem, familiarity breeds confopulation. (*He takes out a notebook and pencil*) Now I'm going to ask you a few questions if you don't mind or if you do mind.

Mike Right.

Rouse How much do you earn?

Mike Oh!

Rouse I shall have your answer checked.

Mike Fifteen thousand.

Rouse Phew! That's a lot of money.

Mike It's not a lot by ——

Rouse Then let's round that down to twelve thousand, shall we? A thousand pounds a month should be ample for anyone outside ·Council offices.

Mike Mr Rouse, I'm sure the Council don't intend you to cut ——

Rouse Who knows what the Council intend, Pemmy? The Council works in strange and wondrous haberdobberies. The fact is that by adjusting your salary from fifteen to twelve thousand, we save twenty per cent.

Mike This is some kind of joke, isn't it?

Rouse Joke? You are talking to a representative of the Council.

Mike Look, I don't mind you investigating how we spend Council money, but there'll be no cuts in salary either for myself or for my staff.

Rouse Mummy, Mummy, I want all the cake, not just a slice! Oh dear, what a kerbaddle. You remind me, Pemmy, of the man with the bag of gold in the sinking boat. "Throw some out!" cried the voice of reason. "No!" cried the voice of greed. And do you know what happened?

Mike No.

Rouse He bubbulated.

Mike He what?

Rouse Now, I must ask you some questions about this establishment of yours. Firstly, what exactly does it do?

Mike It's a theatre.

Rouse That's what it is. I want to know what it does.

Mike Our main activity is to put on plays.

Rouse Plays.

Mike Yes.

Rouse And what do you mean by plays?

Mike Dramas. We range from Shakespeare to modern plays, musicals, pantomime, lunchtime theatre ——

Rouse Are you doing this deliberately?

Mike What?

Rouse Shakespeare, mantopime, sumicals! You can't fuzzle me, Pem, I know the meaning of the word "play", and I doubt whether Sir Charles and the Council will be very pleased to hear that the money extangulated from the tax-payer is now being "played" with.

Mike Mr Rouse, do you actually know what a theatre is?

Rouse That, Pemmy, is what I'm here to find out.

Mike You mean you've never heard of Shakespeare?

Rouse It might be more relevant to ask whether Shakespeare has heard of me.

Mike He died in 1616.

Rouse In that case, he can write in for a rebate.

Mike Tell me, Mr Rouse, since you know absolutely nothing about the theatre, how can you possibly advise me on the best way to run it?

Rouse Oh dear. Oh dear, oh dear, oh dear. The Layman's Blunder. Reorganastification, Pem, is always done by outsiders. When the economy's in a mess, they make the Minister of Education Chancellor of the Exchequer. When education's in a mess, they give it to the Minister of Transport. And every so often, in any case, the Prime Minister does a hey-diddly-plunkyrole which he calls a reshuffle to make sure nobody knows that they're talking about. The outsider sees most, Pemmy. On my last assignment I saved the Council millions because I had no preconstipations.

Mike What was the assignment?

Rouse Hospitals. Do you know what I found in the hospitals, Pem?

Mike No.

Rouse Hundreds and hundreds of people lying in bed. In their pyjamas. Doing absolutely nothing. The Council was paying millions to have these malabiddles fed, warmed, finglepotted at every whimsy by salaried attendants … It was a disgrace.

Mike What did you do?

Rouse I removed a large number of beds, reduced the staff of attendants, and brought in a few hundred supervisors from the Council to stop the malabiddling.

Mike My God!

Rouse You'd be amazed what people get up to. Take the unifarcities.

Mike The what?

Rouse They're connected with education. What did I find there? Huge buildings, rooms, paphernomiums everywhere, hugely expensive. And what were people doing there? Talking and reading. That's it. Talking and reading! I'd have closed them down on the spot.

Mike What happened?

Rouse Sir Charles said some people might complain if we closed them down, so we're just giving them less money and calling it reallocation. Eventually they'll fade away, and then we can put all those huge buildings to some useful purpose, which brings me most aptly to this building here.

Mike Oh God!

Rouse I am not impressed, Pem, with what I see. Before our appointed time of one o'clock, I entered this building incognifariously and looked into some of your rooms. They were empty. Nature, Pem, abhors vacuum cleaners. And so does the Council. This building is full of vacuum cleaners.

Mike Well, there is an explanation for that ...

Rouse Of course. There's an explanation for everything. The hospitals "explained" that all their malabiddles were ill. I laughed. I pointed out to them that the iller a person is, the less value he is to society and the Council, and we are better off without such paracetemols. As for the unifarcities, they "explained" that all their loafylugs were learning. I laughed again. I said it looked to me as if all their loafylugs were loafylugging, and I could learn a darn sight more climbing up a saparony. They had no reply to that. Well now, Pemmy, amuse me with your explanation.

Mike The reason why most of our rooms are empty is that it's lunchtime. People have gone to lunch.

Rouse Go on.

Mike That's the explanation.

Rouse Ho ho ho. You caught me there. I was still *waiting* for the explanation. The rooms are empty because people have gone to lunch.

Mike Exactly.

Rouse Rooms, Pemmy, are always empty because people have gone somewhere. When the people who've gone to lunch return to their rooms, the rooms where they went will then be empty, so what will you tell me? Ah, you'll say, those rooms are empty because the people have gone back to the rooms they weren't in before. This is the merry-go-round of logometrics, Pemmy, and I think you've met your match.

Mike Mr Rouse, I wouldn't dream of crossing logi... logimetric swords with you, but the point is that the main period of activity in a theatre is the evening.

Rouse Ah! So all this space is wasted for the rest of the day.

Mike Mr Rouse, no theatre in the world puts on plays twenty-four hours a day.

Rouse What a good argument. We waste our space, but so does everybody else and so it's all right.

Mike We're not wasting space!

Rouse Sorry! I'm wrong! You're not wasting space! No siree, as they say over the water.

Mike Thank you.

Rouse You're not wasting space. The Council is, by paying for all these vacuum cleaners. And furthermore — (*he turns towards the audience*) — by providing seats for yet more situponners. Oh, yes, I've noticed we're not alone in this room. (*He addresses the audience*) Why aren't you working? Sitting there like dummisuckles. Shouldn't you be filling those vacuum cleaners and doing something useful, instead of situponning and loafylugging? (*He approaches Mavis*) You, for instance, flaunting all your tittibits here in public, does your employer know that you've left the office, or your husband that you're not in the kitchen?

Mavis Mind your own business.

Rouse Oh! I see. (*He returns to Mike*) So that's the kind of behaviour you encourage in your establishment. Rudeness to a member of the Council.

Mike She was certainly no ruder to you than you were to her.

Rouse Are you uppitysoppering her against myself?

Mike She was entirely within her rights.

Rouse Totty botty! Entirely within her rights! But I suppose this was only to be expected after the dreadful experience I had just before meeting you.

Mike What experience?

Rouse When I went to the room known as the Green Room.

Mike What about the Green Room?

Rouse It's not green.

Mike Well, no, but …

Rouse It doesn't bother me. You can call it the pinkyponkypanky room as far as I'm concerned. What bothered me was what I found there. Now, guess what I found.

Mike It was empty.

Rouse On the contrary. It was full. Of men and women watching one man and one woman shouting at each other. The violence of the abuse made it clear that they were husband and wife. And the others were listening to this conversation, and in my presence one young man had the sheer novakarasnikov to call out "Well done" when the woman told the man he was a bloody panda. Of course I left immediately.

Mike They were actors, Mr Rouse. They were rehearsing a play that is to be performed on this very stage later today. I was just checking the set when you came in.

Rouse Actors.

Mike Yes.

Rouse Well, two of them were active. The rest looked passive to me, apart from the idiot who said "Well done".

Mike Mr Rouse, may I explain to you what happens in a play?

Rouse Please do. I'm eager to learn. That's what I'm here for, to learn and to listen ——

Mike Good.

Rouse —— because one learns more from listening, Pemmy, than from talking. You'll find that people who talk too much are invaripocably ignorant. Listening is the secret, and I can assure you, Pemmy, that if you listen to what I have to tell you, we shall double the effipocity of your theatre in no time.

Mike Can I tell you about plays?

Rouse Well if you can't, Mr Pemberton-Hawkesley, then who can? (*Pleased with his little joke*) Ha ho ha he ho!

Mike A play is a story written in dialogue — that's people talking.

Rouse I know what dialogue is, Pemmy. I talk dialogue myself.

Mike Some might call yours monologue. Actors learn the dialogue, and pretend to be the characters in the story. The man and woman in the Green Room weren't really shouting at each other — they were pretending to shout.

Rouse Well, well, well. I wonder, Pemmy, if you could shout for me, and then pretend to shout, so that I can hear the difference.

Mike There's no difference in the sound – only in the situation. It's not the actors who are shouting, but the characters that they're pretending to be.

Rouse You're not a psychambulist, are you, Pem? You're not dibbling in the occult here?

Mike No! Look, somebody else writes the words, the actors learn them ——

Rouse There's no need to adopt that tone.

Mike What tone?

Rouse Of intollyfabulance. What you're telling me is nothing new. We have the same process with Council regulations.

Mike What have Council regulations got to do with it?

Rouse "I promise to put the Council's interests before everyone else's. I promise to spend the Council's money wisely, and not to let anyone else spend it at all. I promise to love, honour and bootismooch Sir Charles and all other Council officials who are above me in the Council hierarchy." Oh yes, Pemmy, I know what's meant by speaking somebody else's words. What I want to know is why.

Mike Why what?

Rouse Why a man and a woman should pretend to be husband and wife, and pretend to shout obscrofications written by somebody else.

Mike You mean the purpose of theatre? To entertain, to excite, to illuminate …

Rouse I'm sorry to contradict you, Pemmy, but I can assure you that what I saw and heard in your Green Room was neither entertaining, nor exciting, nor illuminating. Listening to words that I can hear, alas, every day in my own living-room, not to mention the living-room of the house next door, is frankly dismogrifying.

Mike It's human nature to enjoy seeing how others live. Through the theatre you can watch other people who are different from you ——

Rouse Pem, I watch other people who are different from me all the time. Everyone I know is different from me.

Mike But you can't watch their stories in just a couple of hours, can you?

Rouse I don't want to watch their stories at all, thank you. I've got enough troubles of my own.

Mike But you're involved in your troubles.

Rouse Oh, thank you for telling me!

Mike In the theatre you can watch without being involved. You get the experience without the pain.

Rouse In the immortal words of Praxitateles: "Who needs it, baby?" Life, Pemmy, is for living, not watching. If all your theatre can do is provide gogglisump for Peeping Tomcats, then the sooner we close you down, the better.

Mike Look, hundreds and thousands of people come to our plays!

Rouse Hundreds and thousands of people like alcohol and tobacco, but does that mean the Council must pay out millions to smokers and drinkers?

Mike May I ask what, in your almighty judgement, the Council *should* pay for?

Rouse Certainly. First and foremost they should and fortunately do pay for those whose prime purpose in life is to save the Council money. Which brings me to the future of your theatre.

Mike Oh!

Rouse Do you know what I have decided to do with it, Pemmy?

Mike I suppose you're going to close it.

Rouse No, no, I shall keep it open.

Mike (*with sigh of relief*) Thank you!

Rouse I shall keep it open, and use it for storage.

Mike Storage?

Rouse What better way to utumcabulate all this space than with twenty-four-hours-a-day storage?

Mike You can't do that!

Rouse Storage, Pemmy, is one of the major problems of our age. I myself have a three-bedroomed semi-detached house, and all three bedrooms, not to mention the living-room and the downstairs dobble-de-doo are filled to overflowing just with files. Sometimes my wife and I can't even see each other for files, which is just as well if you knew my wife. Now think how many files you could get into this room alone, Pemmy; it could be the beginning of a storage and theatre revolution.

Mike You're out of your bloody mind!

Rouse And I've heard that before! Of course they said Stephen Potter was mad when he invented the wheel, and Garibaldi when he said the earth went round the sun, and Grizzly P. Vandervold who said money was more important than people, but they were all proved right in the end. Storage, Pemmy — a brand new form of theatre.

Mavis, in the auditorium, produces a gun and fires it at Rouse

Rouse falls

Mavis steps on to the stage

Mavis The unutterable swine. Is he dead?
Rouse Help!
Mike No.

Mavis shoots Rouse again

Mavis I couldn't let it go on. I just couldn't. What must you be thinking?
Mike I'm thinking you might have saved my theatre.
Mavis I don't normally go round shooting people. I'm a very nice person. I belong to Greenpeace. But Mr Pemberton-Hawkesley, I couldn't let him close your theatre.
Mike Of course you couldn't.
Mavis My name is Raquel Bardot. Well, actually, it's Mavis Dinwiddy, but Raquel Bardot is my professional name. I'm an actress. Resting. I love the theatre. And especially this theatre. Your theatre.
Rouse Help!

Mavis casually shoots Rouse again then continues the conversation as if nothing had happened

Mavis I overheard his threats, and something snapped.
Mike (*eyeing Mavis's ample bosom*) Really?
Mavis I lost control, and suddenly I've become — oh God! — a murderess. What's to happen to me?

Mike Well, I don't know.

Mavis In saving you, I may have ruined my life. Oh! Oh! Oh!

Mike Yes, it is a bit awkward.

Mavis What are you going to do with me?

Mike I suppose I ought to send for the police.

Rouse Help!

Mavis Die, you Council dog! (*She shoots Rouse again*) He mustn't live. If he lives, then all is lost. What you're doing in this theatre is wonderful. I've seen all your productions, many times over. I think you're a genius. No, don't protest. It's true. I would give everything I have — absolutely everything — to be ... directed by you. Now tell me, what do you want from me?

Mike Erm ... Well — the body's the problem.

Mavis (*shocked*) What's wrong with it?

Mike No, I meant *his* body.

Mavis Ah!

Mike You couldn't just take it away somewhere, could you?

Mavis Not on my own, Michael. I'm only a weak woman.

Mike I don't want to get involved.

Mavis You needn't. There'd be no commitment, Michael. I wouldn't expect that.

Mike Well, if I help you dump the body, I'll be involved, won't I? I suppose I really ought to ring the police.

Rouse Could I say something at this junkum?

Mike Not unless it's helpful and constructive.

Rouse I've been shot. Four times. My condition might be serious. I'd be grateful if you'd send for an ambulance.

Mavis You bastard! You turd! You Philistine! If we send for an ambulance, don't you realize they'll want to know who shot you? And where will that leave me?

Rouse Under arrest. And quite right too. You can't go round shooting Council dignocrats as and when you please.

Mavis Oh can't I? (*She shoots Rouse again*) You see the kind of man he is? He'll close your theatre, and ruin my reputation. Michael, we must dispose of his body together. After which, perhaps you can "dispose" of my body.

Mike I'm a bit uncomfortable about being an accessory to murder.

Mavis Look on it as an investment. By getting rid of him, you save your theatre, the jobs of your staff, and the cultural heritage of Britain. It's a small price to pay. And I'll be beside you, Michael. Or wherever else you want me.

Mike No, I ought to call the police.

Mavis Stay where you are. (*She points the gun at Mike*) There's still one bullet left, and if you call the police, Michael, I shall use it … Not on you — no, I would never deprive the world of your unique genius — but on myself. My life is in your hands, Michael. Will you let me live? (*She holds the gun against her own head*)

Pause

Mike What do you want me to do?

Mavis Oh, Michael!

Mike I mean, about the body.

Mavis So do I.

Mike His body.

Rouse I think it's only fair to warn you that whatever you do with me, I shall report it to the authorpedics, and will ensure that any soiled trousers will be taken down and used in evidence against you.

Mavis raises the gun

It's your last bullet!

Mavis No, not mine. Yours. (*She shoots Rouse again*)

Mike There's something funny about all this. How can a man with five bullets in him ——

Rouse Six.

Mike Six — still be chatting away as if nothing had happened?

Rouse Council officers are indeshootable. Besides — (*he stands up*) we are protected by standard issue bullet-proof vests as invented by Kaiser Wilhelm Montgomery, the Council's very first full-time efficiency expert.

Mike I see.

Mavis Curses!

Rouse Now then, Pem, I'd be obliged if you'd ring for the police so that this young lady can be duly arrested, tortured, tricked into making her confession, and bedded down by the entire constabulary.

Mike gives Rouse a searching look, and goes out

As for you, Miss Dinwiddy, are the bollichromes of true love stirfrying your minkles?
Mavis Oh yes, Mr Rouse.
Rouse Then let it not be said that a Council officer stood in the way of a romantic tuttigrope. Fly to his arms, Miss Dinwiddy, and any other parts you may wish to fly to.
Mavis Thank you, Mr Rouse.

Mavis hurries off

Rouse Now I am alone.
(*Overacting*) O! What a rogue and peasant slave am I:
              Is it not monstrous that this player here,
              But in fiction, in a dream of passion,
              Could force his soul so to his own conceit
              That from her working, all his visage wann'd,
              Tears in his eyes, distraction in's aspect,
              A broken voice, and his whole function suiting
              With forms to his conceit? And all for nothing!
              For Hecub ... oh!
(*To the audience*) I'd forgotten you were there. Still sitting on your botticles, peepytomming your lives away. Well, what do you make of this latest kerbaddle? Shocked, are you? Rousey isn't the ignopotamus you thought he was? Knows all about Shakespeare, and pantomimes, and musicals? So now you're thinking maybe Rousey isn't a Council officer after all, and maybe this whole rigmatiddle has been a practical joke, and the plot is about to take an unexpected twist. Well, you go on thinking what you want to think. But let me tell you this: we of the Council always know more than you think we know. For instance, you may

believe that Mr Pemberton-Hawkesley, having telephoned the police, is now tinkybinking Miss Dinwiddy. The truth, however, is that he won't have telephoned the police at all. He will have telephoned somebody else. The tinkybinky bit's true, of course, but do you know who Miss Dinwiddy really is? Ah! Now while you ponder that canonder, and while we wait for Mr Pemberton-Hawkesley and Miss Dinwiddy to return, I'm going to ask you some questions. Have you made a full, open and honest declaration of all your earnings to the Inland Revenue? Have you had, are you having, or are you dreaming of having extra-marital sexual relations? Have you driven at more than thirty miles per hour in a built-up area, or more than seventy on a motorway? Have you elastified your business expenses, declaring journeys not made, meals not eaten, beds not slept in? Have you walked through the Green Channel with smugglies tucked away in your case? And have you ever snicked a ball to the wicket-keeper and pretended you never touched it? Repent ye, for the kingdom of the Council is at hand.

Mike and Mavis return, somewhat dishevelled

Rouse Ah, the return of the tinkybinkers. Well, Pem, are the police on their way?

Mike Erm — no.

Rouse No? Did you say no?

Mike I didn't ring them.

Rouse You surprise me, Pem. (*He directs an "I-told-you-so" expression towards the audience*) But did you make a phone call.

Mike Yes.

Rouse You rang the Council.

Mike Yes.

Rouse People always do. And you had a nasty shock.

Mike Yes.

Rouse Because you'd been hoping, like many a nonnyloop before you, that I was not who I said I was.

Mike Yes.

Rouse But I am.

Mike Yes.

Rouse And at this junkum you were joined by Miss Dinwiddy.

Mike Yes.

Rouse I am shocked. Miss Dinwiddy, tell me in your own words precisely what happened.

Mavis I joined Mr Pemberton-Hawkesley, Mr Rouse, and then Mr Pemberton-Hawkesley joined me.

Rouse Shocking. I am shocked. And Mrs Pemberton-Hawkesley will also be shocked. If she finds out.

Mike Oh God!

Rouse Now Pem, this matter of turning your theatre into a storage diponium. Can I take it that you will not oppose the Council's decision?

Mike I won't oppose it.

Rouse What wonderful news. A triumph of co-operation and tinkybinking. I in turn will refrain from telephoning Mrs Pemberton-Hawkesley.

Mike Thank you.

Rouse Meanwhile, Miss Dinwiddy, there is the little matter of your attempted murder of my good self.

Mavis Oh!

Rouse Which I am honour bound to report to the police.

Mavis Oh dear!

Rouse Unless you care to accompany me to a lonely spot where I can take full advantage of your boobicosity.

Mavis Oh!

Rouse Does that mean yes or no?

Mavis Yes.

Rouse Another rung in the great ladder of Council progress. Goodbye, Pem. It's been a pleasure to have you listen to me, and to be able to save your theatre so footlightedly.

Rouse takes Mavis's hand. They head towards the exit, but stop

Oh! Miss Dinwiddy, before we depart, these silent googlepeeps would like to know who you really are. Perhaps you could tell them?

Mavis I'm Raquel Bardot, the actress.
Rouse Resting?
Mavis Resting.
Rouse (*to the audience*) Work that one out.

Black-out

FURNITURE AND PROPERTY LIST

Personal: **Rouse**: notebook and pencil
Mavis: gun (loaded with six blanks)

Samuel French is grateful to Charles Vance, Vice- Chairman of the Theatres Advisory Council, for the following information regarding the Firearms (Amendment) Bill:

"The Firearms (Amendment) Bill does not affect blank-firing pistols which are not readily convertible (i.e. those which do not require a Firearms Certificate). Among the reasons against imposing restrictions on such items is their use in theatre, cinema and television as a "safe" alternative to real guns.

The general prohibition on the possession of real handguns will apply to those used for theatrical purposes. It would clearly be anomalous to prohibit the use of those items for target shooting, but permit their use for purposes where a fully-working gun is not needed. As handguns will become "Section 5" prohibited weapons, they would fall under the same arrangements as at present apply to real machine guns. As you will know, there are companies which are authorised by the Secretary of State to supply such weapons for theatrical purposes.

The exemption under Section 12 of the Firearms Act 1968, whereby actors can use firearms without themselves having a Firearms Certificate, will remain in force".

Regulations apply to the United Kingdom only. Producers in other countries should refer to appropriate legislation.

LIGHTING PLOT

Practical fittings required: nil
One interior. The same throughout

To open: General interior lighting

Cue 1   **Rouse**: "Work that one out."   (Page 16)
            Black-out

EFFECTS PLOT

No cues

www.ingramcontent.com/pod-product-compliance
Ingram Content Group UK Ltd.
Pitfield, Milton Keynes, MK11 3LW, UK
UKHW021819150726
7214IPUK00017B/200